BRISTOL FIRST

city of discovery, invention and enterprise

John Sansom

redcliffe

First published in 1997 by Redcliffe Press
of Bristol and Tiverton

© John Sansom

British Library Cataloguing in Publication Data
A catalogue record for this book is available from
The British Library

ISBN 1 900178 90 7

Redcliffe Press,
Halsgrove House,
Lower Moor Way,
Tiverton, Devon EX16 6SS
Tele: 01884 243242
Fax 01884 243325

Printed in England by Hillman Printers (Frome) Ltd

Contents

Bristol First

No one is more zealous than the convert. Like so many others, I came to Bristol from outside, fell under its spell and now wouldn't want to live anywhere else. In putting some of this into *Bristol First*, I don't attempt to explain the magic – that ambition is for another day – but I do offer a sort of scrapbook, a collection of snap-shots of some of the bits that contribute to the whole picture. So this is a partial record, in two senses of the word, personal and eccentrically shaped.

For many years, Bristol has played a second fiddle to nearby Bath as a magnet for visitors. It was a preference not shared by the late John Betjeman, who once wrote that despite the damage inflicted on it by Hitler's bombs (and, he might have added, by post-war planners), Bristol remained the finest city in England. Like Betjeman, I have always preferred Bristolians' proud but more work-a-day attitude to what has been passed on to them by previous generations.

Bristol's famed conservatism, if sometimes infuriating, saved it from the worst excesses of the 1960s and 1970s, when it narrowly avoided being wrecked by the road-builders. But things are changing. Bristol now positively embraces the benefits that come from a healthy tourist trade, and unlike some of the smaller 'heritage' towns which must sometimes rue their fame, it is large enough to welcome visitors without being overwhelmed by them. And with the imaginative schemes taking shape on Harbourside epitomising a new optimism, Bristol's immediate future is as exciting as its colourful past.

Bristol First is therefore aimed both at the resident who'd like to know a bit more, and at the visitor who may know next to nothing of what the city has to offer. The device I have adopted is the simple one of bringing together some of the claims to uniqueness, or discovery, or invention or superlative that lie behind the face of modern Bristol. Few will be surprised to find in these pages the now much-exposed John Cabot, or St Mary Redcliffe, that paragon of church architecture, or the living memorials to the genius of Isambard Kingdom Brunel. But the number of 'firsts' which can be claimed for Bristol will come as a surprise, even if I have indulged personal whims by including a couple of minor sporting and literary events. As it is, I have left out many, concentrating in the main on the visual. This inevitably leaves out whole areas of endeavour which can perhaps be more properly celebrated elsewhere – from, for example, the achievement of Bristol-born Elizabeth Blackwell in becoming the first woman to qualify and register as a doctor in 1849 to the marvellous modern pioneering work done in Bristol hospitals.

Because this is not an attempt to define, or even to paint a rounded picture, the reader will find some imbalances. The few hundred words given to the architectural wonders of Bristol Cathedral should not be weighed against the disproportionate space given to the cricketing achievement of a thirteen-year old schoolboy one halcyon summer a hundred years ago. But for anyone wanting to know more about Bristol's teeming history, there is a rich literature, to which Redcliffe Press alone has contributed something over 120 volumes. Some of these are suggested for further reading. Better still, many of the 'firsts' can be visited or seen in the city's wonderful galleries and museums.

I hope *Bristol First* will whet a few thousand appetites and encourage a fuller discovery of this great European city.

John Sansom, May, 1997.

Acknowledgements

My main debt of gratitude is to the writers of the books of local history which Redcliffe Press have published in the past twenty years. It is largely through reading, editing and publishing their invaluable work that I have acquired the background knowledge to underpin my own experience and observation of the many-sided life of this immensely rewarding city.

More recently, I have been helped by Sharon Butler of Strategy PR, Etienne de Coensel of NatWest Insurance Services, Gareth Griffiths of the British Empire & Commonwealth Museum, Lawrence Gunn of John Wesley's Chapel, Maggie Johnson of Royal Mail, Andrew Kelly of the Bristol Cultural Development Partnership, Sue Lion of Wildscreen, Lynn Lynch of the s.s. Great Britain Project, Jan Lyons of The Exploratory, Tim Martienssen of Arnolfini, Martin Miller of Bristol City Museums and Art Gallery, Alan Noble of Cameron Balloons Ltd., and Penny Samuel of the Bristol International Balloon Fiesta.

Some of the illustrations have come from previous Redcliffe commissions, or have been kindly supplied by institutions referred to in these pages. As ever, Bristol City Museums & Art Gallery have been a helpful source, and I should like also to thank Cedric Barker for allowing the use of his photographs of Clifton Cathedral, Clifton College, the Observatory and the Clifton Suspension Bridge, the National Portrait Gallery for the picture of Sarah Siddons and the Tate Gallery for Henry Wallis' 'Death of Chatterton', Stuart Culling for help with photographs of the Balloon Festival, Colin Sanger for the 'Matthew'; and in particular Fiona Sansom for her special 'takes' of Temple Church, the nails, the Exchange clock, Eugenie House and the memorials to John Cabot, Edward Colston, Samuel Plimsoll, William III and Woodes Rogers. **JS**

Bristol's Discovery of America

There's little doubt – at least in the minds of loyal Bristolians – that mainland America was discovered by intrepid sailors from Bristol.

If it wasn't John Cabot's band of seafarers in 1497, then it was even earlier Bristol mariners who, denied access to Icelandic waters and seeking new cod fisheries, first sighted what we now call Newfoundland – well before poor old Columbus stumbled ashore on an island in the West Indies.

Unfortunately, hard evidence is difficult to come by. What is known for sure is that John Cabot set out from Bristol in May, 1497 in the *Matthew* – like Columbus, in search of a new route to Asia. After thirty-five days, the small contingent of sailors reached the North American continent, planted the flags of the English king Henry VII and the Pope, beat a hasty retreat after seeing tell-tale signs of habitation and spent the next month exploring the coastline. No one knows for sure where exactly they landed – on what is now Newfoundland or further south, possibly as far as Maine.

Back in England, Cabot sought another audience with the king. Convinced he had reached Asia and with it the promise of easier access to the spices and other treasures of the East, he persuaded Henry to back a larger expedition. Five ships set out from Bristol the following year, sailing, as far as the history books are concerned, to oblivion. There is no record of any returning to England, and the expedition's fate is shrouded in mystery. Experts, though, reckon it highly unlikely that all five

The replica Matthew, *built to recreate Cabot's historic voyage of discovery.*

ships could have been lost at sea.

So were the party murdered by hostile natives? Or, as seems increasingly likely as snippets of fresh evidence emerge, did they explore extensively down the eastern American coastline, only to be killed by Spanish pirates?

John Cabot on the Arnolfini quayside.

One eminent nineteenth-century Spanish historian offers this tantalizing possibility in his definitive history of the Spanish voyages of discovery: 'It is certain that Hojeda in his first [1499] expedition encountered certain Englishmen in the vicinity of Coquibacoa.' If this is so, they were almost definitely members of Cabot's 1498 expedition.

Even more tantalizing is the evidence of Juan de la Cosa's map of the world in 1500, which clearly depicts five English flags along the north and central American coastline. So there is circumstantial evidence that Cabot at least made it to America a second time, and there is even a school of thought which argues that he returned safely from that trip and continued to put to sea into the sixteenth century.

But one point on which most Bristolians would surely agree is how America got its name. The conventional wisdom long attributed this to Amerigo Vespucci, the tall story-telling voyager whose name became associated with the New World in a 1507 map. But it is not only local sentiment that suggests Bristol has the stronger claim. For the customs collector and Bristol merchant responsible for paying Cabot's £20 pension from Henry VII was none other than Richard Ameryk (or Americ, as it was spelt on his merchant's mark). Known for his generous spirit – he once promised to name an island after his barber – it is no great speculation that Cabot chose to immortalise his benefactor by naming the discovered territory after him.

In *John Cabot and The Matthew*, author Ian Wilson goes further. Might not the unworthy Vespucci have seen a now vanished chart from Cabot's 1498 expedition with the place name 'America' and, noting the similarity with his own first name, decided to adopt it as his own invention? Whatever the truth, it surely is at the very least an astonishing coincidence.

But why does Columbus, who after all found only the islands of the West Indies on his voyage in 1492, get all the glory? It helps to have a profile. John Cabot has almost none – no portrait has survived, no letters, no diary entries. Even his son, Sebastian, apparently left no memoir of his father or his exploits.

There is no doubt that had Cabot definitely returned from the 1498 expedition with documentary and physical evidence, his name would rank with that of his fellow Italian. As it is, we are left with only scraps. A piece of paper confirming he rented a house in St Nicholas Street. Details of his pension. The rib of a cow whale hanging in St Mary Redcliffe church, and reputedly a relic from his first voyage.

Otherwise, the Cabot 'memorabilia' in Bristol is of more recent origin. The striking Cabot Tower on Brandon Hill was erected at the end of the nineteenth century to mark the 400th anniversary of his successful voyage. A few years later, in 1906, local artist Ernest Board painted a splendidly colourful, if historically dubious, reconstruction of Cabot's departure from a Bristol quayside. This hangs in the City Museum & Art Gallery in Queen's Road. Down in the harbour, a modern sculpture of a lugubrious Cabot can been seen at the waterfront outside Arnolfini.

But the most magnificent reminder of Cabot and Bristol's early years of exploration is the replica *Matthew*, which graced the 1996 International Festival of the Sea in Bristol in preparation for its voyage in May, 1997 to St John's Harbour in Newfoundland five hundred years after the original sailing. It is impossible to say exactly what Cabot's ship looked like, but the new *Matthew's* design is based on a detailed analysis of what is known of ships of the period. After a tour of the eastern seaboard of the United States, she is then scheduled to return to a permanent berth in Bristol at the Matthew Visitor Centre on Redcliffe Wharf, to play host in the coming year to millions of tourists attracted to the city and its great maritime heritage.

S.S. Great Britain

The greatest ship the world had ever seen

It's hard to believe, now – but there were serious doubts about the wisdom of allowing Isambard Kingdom Brunel's great ship into Bristol when she was brought back from the Falkland Islands in an audacious rescue operation a quarter of a century ago.

The more cautious city fathers may have agonized, but their citizens didn't. Thousands lined the Avon Gorge and dockside in July, 1970 to give the *s.s. Great Britain* an emotional welcome back, 126 years after she had last sailed the Avon waters. Legend already has it that the cry 'Save her, save her' rose from the thronging crowds as the battered hulk was edged cautiously back towards the original dry dock in which she had been built in the early 1840s.

Brunel's grand old ship, still being painstakingly restored to her former glory, is now one of Bristol's great tourist attractions. Already more than three million visitors have squeezed through the turnstiles to step on board the most revolutionary ship of her time. She was the first ocean-going propeller-driven iron ship in history, forsaking the timber hull and paddle wheels of her immediate predecessor, the *s.s. Great Western*, also designed by Brunel and built in Bristol Docks.

The *Great Britain* was then the largest ship in the world, her dimensions at the time a staggering 322 feet long, weighing almost 3000 tons and capable of carrying 130 crew and up to 360 passengers. Much modified over the years, she plied the Atlantic until 1852, made 32 round voyages from Liverpool to Melbourne and, in 1861, carried the first All-England cricket team to visit Australia. She also carried troops to the Crimea and to India, and was finally converted to a cargo ship before being abandoned in the Falkland Islands – but not until she had travelled more than a million sea miles.

Brunel's first link with Bristol was the competition to design the Clifton Suspension Bridge which he entered as a young man. But he came to be designing steam ships in Bristol as a natural – as he saw it – extension of the rail link he had helped forge between London and Bristol. Why stop at Bristol? Why not just carry on across the ocean to New York? This breathtaking idea epitomised the vision of the greatest engineer of his time. And so the *s.s. Great Western*, built at what is now Prince's Wharf – a plaque near the Industrial Museum marks the spot – was launched in 1838 and was only narrowly beaten by a Liverpool rival to the honour of making the first westward steam-powered crossing of the Atlantic.

The *Great Britain* was conceived as a sister ship to provide a regular shuttle service for passengers and goods. Sadly, for practical and financial reasons, the two great ships soon severed their links with Bristol, and spent much of their working lives plying from Liverpool. The grand London to New York service via Bristol never materialised, but a legacy remains in the shape of Brunel House, not far from College Green, which was built as the Royal Western Hotel and opened in 1839 to accommodate passengers en route from Brunel's Temple Meads railway station to the waiting ship. The building was later converted into Turkish baths and now houses offices.

Restoration work on the s.s. *Great Britain* is administered by a charity specially set up for the purpose. One of the great attractions for visitors is Brunel's great engine which is currently being reconstructed on board as part of the programme. Entrance fees are spent in support of the ship, which can be visited every day of the year except Christmas and Boxing Day. Depending on the time of year, the normal opening hours are 10am-4.30 or 5.30pm. Admission charge. The magnificent, fully restored dining saloon is open to the public, and can be hired for banquets and wedding receptions.

The adjoining Maritime Heritage Centre on Wapping Wharf tells the fuller story of shipbuilding in Bristol, and is also open daily. Further along the waterfront, more maritime history, including models of Bristol's early ships, is on offer at the Industrial Museum near Prince Street bridge.

The Industrial Museum is open: April 1-October 31 Sat-Wed, 10am-5pm; Nov 1-March 31 Sat and Sun, 10am-5pm. Admission charge (except for leisure card-holders, children under 16 and full time students).

Brunel's great ship undergoing restoration in her original dry dock.

Another Brunel masterpiece in Bristol is the original Temple Meads railway station built for the Bristol end of his Great Western Railway system from Paddington to the west. It was for his visionary railway concept, as well as his three great ships – the mighty *s.s. Great Eastern*, built in London, was the third of

The original GWR terminus at Temple Meads.

the triumvirate – that Isambard Kingdom Brunel became truly a legend in his own lifetime.

The building, with its imposing neo-Tudor facade at the bottom of the incline which leads to the present railway station, was built in 1839-41 and today stands largely unchanged as the oldest surviving railway terminus in the world. Its crowning feature is the immense mock hammer-beam roof supported on arcades of Tudor arched iron columns.

The Brunel station has not been used as such since 1965. After various restoration works, the complex is used today partly as a car park, exhibition area and is the present home of the 'hands on' Exploratory science centre, before its proposed move to the new Harbourside site. The Empire & Commonwealth Museum is also housed here.

As something of an anti-climax to the great engineer's living monuments around the city, a bronze statue of Brunel can be seen outside the Bristol & West Building Society's headquarters at Broad Quay. The society also commissioned the rather more impressive, seated, memorial at Paddington railway station. The two works, by sculptor John Doubleday, were unveiled within hours of each other in May, 1982. A third Doubleday statue paid for by Bristol & West – of the comic genius, Charlie Chaplin – stands in London's Leicester Square.

Bristol Leads in 'Hands-on' Science

The idea behind Britain's first 'hands-on' science centre at the Exploratory – to make learning fun by doing instead of just looking – goes back more than 350 years to the scientist and philosopher Francis Bacon. In his unfinished book *New Atlantis*, published after his death in 1627, he described an imaginary science centre called the House of Salomon, designed for both amusement and serious, practical investigation of scientific phenomena.

The Bristol Exploratory was the first such centre in the UK when it opened in 1984, and was modelled on one established in San Francisco in the late 1960s. The prime mover in Bristol was Professor Richard Gregory of Bristol University, who is now chairman of the board of trustees.

Over 150 exhibits on two floors at Brunel's original 1840 GWR terminus at Temple Meads encourage not just children, but all the family, to learn how things work the practical way. Visitors can make an arch-bridge to stand on, generate electricity or touch a tornado. From lasers to lenses, everything is hands-on. The Stradivarium music and sound gallery includes the world's largest guitar.

Open: daily 10am-5pm. Admission charge.

Temple Meads is the last of the Exploratory's short-term homes, as the centre is scheduled to move to Harbourside where Science World will be one of the Bristol 2000 projects taking the city into the new millenium.

Eager to learn at Bristol's Exploratory.

First for Study of Empire

The Empire & Commonwealth Museum taking shape at Temple Meads will take an objective look at the British Empire as it was, 'warts and all'. Bristol's central role in world exploration from Cabot's day – and its less-than-glorious involvement in the slave trade – make it an appropriate venue for the first purely historical museum of its kind.

Permanent and changing displays will trace the remarkable story of how Britain became the centre of a vast empire which in its own right and through the spread of the English language has had a momentous influence on the course of world history.

An 1846 lithograph of Brunel's great terminus, which will house the museum.

Bristol Blue Glass

Bristol Blue – that intensely coloured and much coveted glass that bears the city's name – is unique, and yet it isn't.

The glowing blue of the antique specimens displayed in dealers' cabinets and in Bristol drawing rooms comes from smalt, a vitreous form of cobalt – the colouring agent used for glass and ceramics which the Bristol and Plymouth porcelain manufacturer, William Cookworthy managed to acquire when the Royal Saxony works closed down in 1763.

But although much Bristol blue glass was made in the city, Cookworthy had also sold the smalt to glassmakers elsewhere – so the glass which bears the Bristol name is not unique to the area. But some fine decanters and other ware can definitely be traced to Bristol, signed by the celebrated Isaac Jacobs. Other fine Bristol glass comes in green and amethyst.

Glass making had been a staple industry in Bristol long before the invention of the blue glass, and many fine examples can be seen in the City Museum in Queen's Road and Harveys Wine Museum in Denmark Street. The city was for long the largest glass-making centre outside London. In its heyday, much was made for export to America, as well as for the domestic market. At one time, the Bristol skyline was dotted with the brick cones which housed the furnaces. In a visit to the city in 1739, the poet Alexander Pope wrote of 'twenty odd pyramids smoking over the town'. But they were far from being a quaint tourist attraction, 'the city, from the continual smoke arising from them, being constantly darkened and in dirt, while the inhabitants are almost suffocated with noxious effluvia', as Daniel Defoe wrote early in the eighteenth century.

Things were even worse inside. Writer and educationalist, Hannah More visited a glasshouse and was shocked by what she found. 'The swearing, eating and drinking of these half-dressed, black-looking beings gave a most infernal and horrid appearance. They themselves mockingly called it Botany Bay, or Living Hell.'

Glassmaking in Bristol declined in the nineteenth century, and the last business closed in the 1920s. Only one fragment of the old glasshouses survives – in Prewett Street, Redcliffe, and now incorporated into the Kiln restaurant at the Hilton National Hotel.

A modern form of Bristol blue glass is now made in the city, and is popular with tourists looking for a memento of their visit. Although not quite replicating the almost violet hue of the original, these are attractive items. There are many different pieces, from earrings to ship's decanters, and they can be bought in the excellent City Museum Shop, the Tourist Information Centre and elsewhere.

Finger bowl and dish: Bristol blue glass decorated by the noted Isaac Jacobs, c.1805.

Clifton Suspension Bridge

'The wonder of the age'

Sooner or later, there had to be a bridge over the Avon to join Clifton to Leigh Woods on the Somerset side of the gorge. But Isambard Kingdom Brunel's elegant suspension bridge which now attracts visitors by the thousand every year was completed only after a catalogue of disappointments, and then five years after his death.

The story goes back to 1753 when, in an unlikely gesture, a Bristol wine merchant called William Vick bequeathed £1000 to the care of the Society of Merchant Venturers to be invested until it had grown to £10,000 – enough, he calculated, to build a bridge to join the two sides of the gorge. Just why Vick set his heart on this enterprise is a puzzle: in his day, there were few houses in Clifton and on the other side of the water little but trees and fields.

Such is the power of compound interest that by 1829 the fund had reached £8000. The competition which was then announced attracted 22 entries. Thomas Telford, the eminent engineer and builder of the Menai Bridge, was appointed competition judge and rejected the lot. The trustees, perhaps taking the hint, then invited Telford to submit his own proposals. His bulky design – with massive piers rising from the foot of the gorge – was accepted by the committee and received parliamentary consent, but was not popular with Bristolians and was eventually turned down on grounds of cost.

Even earlier, in the 1790s, William Bridges had produced a fantastic plan for a bridge and miniature village with houses, shops, corn exchange, chapel and offices beneath the proposed roadway spanning the structure. It was totally impracticable and, in any case, the financial crisis precipitated by the Napoleonic Wars killed off the idea.

A second competition was held in October 1830, when the twenty-four-year old Brunel's new design was accepted. His first submission, in the earlier competition, had been rejected on engineering grounds. Even now, there was an abortive start to the new proposal and further financial difficulties, but work finally began in earnest in 1836. The sponsors ran out of cash after seven years – £30,000 short of their £75,000 target and the bridge was abandoned. It then stood forlornly for almost twenty years until, in 1860, by which time Brunel was dead, a further effort was made to complete the project. A new parliamentary act gave the necessary powers, the funds were raised and only four years later crowds estimated at up to 150,000 were turning out to witness the grand ceremonial opening of the great bridge on Thursday, 8 December, 1864 – 110 years after William Vick's initiative and a fitting tribute to the genius of its designer.

Sir Abraham Elton at the turf cutting ceremony back in 1831 had prematurely declared of the young Brunel: 'There will come a time when, as that gentleman walks along the streets or as he passes from city to city, the cry would be raised – "There goes the man who reared that stupendous work, the ornament of Bristol and the wonder of the age".'

The bridge had been Brunel's first individual commission. Although he didn't live to see 'My first child, my

Brunel's 'first child and darling'.

darling' built, his design led to a life-long association with the city, which was later to see much of his great work, the Great Western Railway and two of his ocean-going steam ships.

For the record, Clifton Suspension Bridge has a total length of 1352 feet, a span between piers of 703 feet, stands 245 feet above high water and weighs 1500 tons. A curious statistic is that the main chains vary in length – expanding in the summer sunshine, when they can be up to three inches longer than in the cold of winter. A tribute to Brunel's engineering skills is that a bridge constructed for horse-drawn and foot traffic now carries millions of cars a year.

From the start, it was a magnet for potential suicides, and the first fatality occurred in 1866, since when more than 200 sad souls have perished. There was one celebrated survivor. In 1885, Sarah Ann Henley threw herself off the bridge after a lovers' tiff, did a complete somersault in the air and, to her great disappointment, was gently parachuted by her petticoats into the mud below. She later married, became a grandmother and lived to a great age.

Aircraft have flown under the bridge – the first was piloted by Maurice Tétard, flying a Bristol Boxkite and the second a year later by Sir Alan Cobham. In 1957, a Royal Air Force pilot lost his life when his Vampire jet crashed attempting the hazardous feat at 450 miles an hour. But most of us have been content to stand and marvel at the beautiful structure, take a stroll across or attempt to capture its beauty on film or on canvas.

Just above the bridge on the Clifton downs stands the Observatory – all that remains of a old snuff mill. In 1828, William West rented the mill and installed a camera obscura. These instruments of innocent voyeurism were once all the rage, but Bristol's is one of only a handful of survivors. A mirror in the roof reflects the panorama outside the tower downwards on to a shallow horizontal saucer screen. Its charm was once well described by travel writer, H.V. Morton as 'the illusion it imparts of omnipotence. The people who stroll calmly across the mysterious Merlin's table in the darkened room are deliciously unconscious that the hill has its eye on them. They are so natural that one childishly follows them with a finger and pinches the empty air in a futile attempt to pick them up.' Ah, the magic of a more innocent age!

First for Sherry

It's one of the world's most famous drinks, and yet no one knows for sure how Bristol Milk sherry acquired its name. What is certain, is that toasting visitors in this sweet fortified wine is an age-old Bristol custom.

As early as 1634, a visitor recorded that 'with a cup of Bristow milk, we parted with our honest and grave host and bad this sweet city adieu.' Did this everyday use lead to its household name, or was it that parents introduced their children to it almost as early as their mother's milk?

Even Samuel Pepys had a word for it. The redoubtable diarist recorded a visit to Bristol in June, 1668 when his maid's father 'did give us good entertainment of strawberries, a whole venison pasty and plenty of brave wine, and above all Bristol Milk'. Equally memorable was the aside uttered by the Prince of Wales when tasting the sherry on a visit in 1901. 'Bristol,' he said, 'must have damn fine cows.'

Although it is synonymous with Harveys, this is not a proprietary brand, and other Bristol wine shippers have had their own versions. But the famous Bristol Cream sherry certainly is unique to Harveys. The firm were experimenting with a smoother and less sweet sherry back in the 1860s. It still had no name when a valued customer visiting their Denmark Street cellars was offered a sample of two sherries. 'If this is Milk,' she declared magisterially, 'then *this* is Cream.' So was born today's largest selling sherry in the world.

Edward Ardizzone's recreation of the naming of Bristol Cream sherry.

Sleepy Bristol Plumber Invented Lead Shot Process

Most of us at some time dream of making our fortunes – but for one Bristolian the dream was self-fulfilling.

There are several versions of the story. One has it that Bristol plumber William Watts could not – or maybe dare not – make it home after a long night's drinking in a local tavern, and fell asleep in nearby St Mary Redcliffe churchyard. There, he had a strange dream of molten lead being poured through the holes in a colander into a tank of water. The lead globules hardened as they fell and landed in the water perfectly spherical without flattening on impact.

The following morning, a now sober Watts saw the commercial possibilities. A cheaper manufacture of lead shot, which until then could only be laboriously cast in moulds, could be a great money spinner. He set about gutting his Redcliffe Hill house to make experiments with lead from old Roman workings on Mendip. To achieve the optimum drop for the size of shot required – the longer the fall, the larger the spheres – he added a 50-foot tower to his house, and excavated the cellars into the Redcliffe caves below.

The shot-making process was a triumphant success. In 1782, Watts took out a patent for an improved method 'making small Shot Solid throughout Perfectly globular in Form ...' He later sold out to a local firm for a then massive £10,000.

Watts next turned to property speculation, sinking his fortune in a scheme to build the longest terrace in Bristol, high above the Avon on the Clifton hillside. But what became Windsor Terrace needed an immense retaining wall to stop it sliding into the water below. The cost brought bankruptcy and an early death.

Windsor Terrace, one of Clifton's architectural masterpieces, stands proudly overlooking the city docks, its high retaining wall known as Watts' Folly. But Watts' old house on Redcliffe Hill has gone – a victim of road-widening in 1968. The lead shot process had been continuously carried out in that ramshackled building for nearly 200 years.

The business, by then owned by Sheldon Bush & Patent Shot Company, an ICI subsidiary, then transferred to Cheese Lane. A striking new shot tower was built, to be hailed as one of the city's most interesting new buildings. Although now redundant, this beer barrel atop a concrete pole – as one commentator described it – still dominates the waterfront by St Philip's Bridge.

The Bristol Blanket Myth

There is an enduring, if minor, myth that Bristol can take credit for the 'invention' of the blanket. It's a seductive idea, because Bristol did have a flourishing cloth industry, and one of the leading lights in the weaving community in the Middle Ages was indeed an Edmund Blanket – or Thomas, depending on which account you read.

The claim cannot stand scrutiny, though, as a coarse white cloth had been known, from the French *blanchette*, some centuries earlier. Indeed, Thomas Becket was said to have been dressed in a 'curtil of whit blankit' generations before the Blanket family first appeared in Bristol. So the coincidence is just that, unless the family acquired their name by association with their occupation, as people commonly did in those days.

Edmund Blanket was certainly a Bristol notable. A double effigy of him and his wife marks his burial in St Stephen's Church in 1371. Like all ancient churches, St Stephen's has its share of interesting memorials, including ones to Martin Pring, a notable explorer who discovered Cape Cod in 1603, Sir George Snygge, mayor of Bristol and three times member of parliament, and George Macready Chute, whose inscription reads 'manager of the Prince's Theatre in this city and comedian' and who died aged 37 in 1888.

Notable artefacts in St Stephen's include the wrought ironwork of William Edney, a Bristol craftsman of the late seventeenth century, and a fine eagle lectern dating from the fourteenth century.

Originally on the waterfront, before the Centre was filled in, St Stephen's has been the 'harbour church' since medieval times. Its parish boundaries embrace the river Avon and extend into the Bristol Channel to include the islands of Steep Holm, Flat Holm and Denny.

Bristol's Cinema Pioneer

The inscription on the headstone which Sir Edwin Lutyens designed for William Friese-Greene's grave in Highgate Cemetery in 1921 seemed the final accolade for the Bristol-born photographer. It read: 'William Friese-Greene. The Inventor of Kinematography. His genius bestowed upon humanity the boon of commercial kinematography, of which he was the first inventor and patentee.'

But it was nothing like as simple as that – even if the British cinema industry did give him a great send off. Even today, Friese-Greene's roller-coaster ride to lasting fame shows no sign of stabilising, and few film historians now claim that Friese-Greene was much more than an early experimenter. The balance of evidence has until recently clearly favoured the claim of Thomas Edison, the American inventor, to be the father of cinema. The story of their rivalry is a sad muddle of claims and counter-claims, patent applications and law suits and, for Friese-Greene, bankruptcy and poverty. He collapsed and died after making a speech at a public meeting ironically called to settle a dispute in the film industry. He was found to have less than two shillings in his pockets. And yet, and yet ...

That William Friese-Greene, a successful photographer in Bristol, Bath and London, was experimenting with moving images in the late-1880s is beyond dispute. He did produce a jerky image of sorts of Hyde Park traffic, but a surviving fragment suggests that the sequence of pictures was taken too slowly to show real movement. We may never now know the full story even if, outside

William Friese-Greene: father of the cinema, or just a plucky pioneer?

Bristol, the world has given its verdict: Friese-Greene was barely mentioned during the recent centenary of cinema celebrations.

But it was during research for those very celebrations that a Bristol film-maker turned up some convincing evidence to support Friese-Greene's claim to cinematic fame. Spurred by a remarkable discovery in France, film-maker Peter Carpenter was, as *Bristol First* was being published, actively looking to make a TV documentary about the whole astonishing saga.

In 1955, a plaque was erected at 12 College Street, Bristol to mark Friese-Greene's birth there one hundred years earlier, and a wall tablet was also placed in St George's church on Brandon Hill. When College Street was demolished for a municipal car park – which also saw the last of a house where Coleridge once lived – the plaque was resited at the rear of the Council House. There is another plaque at 67 Queen's Road, where in happier days Friese-Greene took portrait photographs of fashionable Clifton ladies and their families. And then, to keep the pot boiling, yet another memorial was unveiled in March 1997, this time in the theatre at Bristol's Queen Elizabeth's Hospital School to mark the inventor's school-days there.

Friese-Greene had worked doggedly to the end. As part of its recognition of one hundred years of cinema, Arnolfini screened his *Kino – The Girl of Colour*, an experiment with colour film which he made the year before he died, each frame of which was individually hand tinted.

On the day that was shown, November 4th, 1996, Arnolfini unveiled a plaque dedicated to its support of contemporary and world cinema in Bristol.

Whatever his ultimate status in the pantheon of cinema history, William Friese-Greene will always be remembered in Bristol as – at the very least – a plucky pioneer and an extraordinary character – and the only person to have four plaques to his name in the city!

Unlike the continuing debate about William Friese-Greene, there can be no doubt about the cinematic and TV pre-eminence of the Bristol-based creators of the lovable Wallace and Gromit.

Bristolians Peter Lord and David Sproxton's love affair with three-dimensional clay animated characters goes back about twenty years and led to their first big success with 'The Amazing Adventures of Morph'. Nick Park joined them in Aardman Animations in the mid-1980s, since when an impressive list of films to set audiences chuckling throughout the world has included the first Wallace and Gromit adventure, 'A Grand Day Out', the now classic 'The Wrong Trousers', which won a 1994 Oscar for Best Short Animated Film and the (if possible) even funnier 'A Close Shave' which pulled in more BAFTA and Oscar Awards.

This multi-talented Bristol team looks set to produce more prize-winning masterpeices – whether TV commercials, children's series or videos – in the years to come.

Bristol's Art Nouveau Palaces

To students of architecture, and the more casual visitor, Bristol's great feature is its wealth of Georgian and Regency architecture. But it also boasts two fine examples of art nouveau.

A few yards from St John's Arch in Broad Street stands a fantastic creation by Bristol's most visionary printer, Edward Everard. Designed by architect Henry Williams and built in 1900-01 as a printing works, the building's crowning glory is the facade of white faience and highly coloured Doulton Carrara ware designed by W.J. Neatby, of the Doulton works in Lambeth.

The design of the building, with its round-headed arches with broad gable and small turrets above, was intended to reflect the nearby St John's Arch – but there any similarity ends. What makes this such a remarkable and important building is the exuberance of the decorative treatment.

The decoration commemorates two great figures: Gutenberg, who invented the process of printing from moveable metal type in the fifteenth century, and William Morris, Socialist and artist-craftsman who led a late-nineteeth century revival of fine printing. The eagle-eyed will spot the spelling mistake in Gutenburg's name on the facade. The angelic figure between the two pioneers symbolises the Spirit of Literature presiding over ancient and modern printing; above, is another allegorical figure holding a lamp and mirror, representing light and truth. Everard's own name appears below in the type face he himself designed.

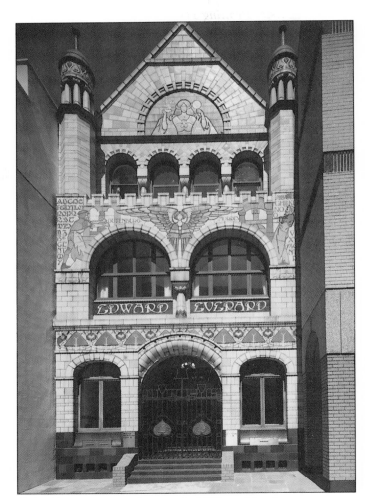

Bristol's art nouveau homage to William Morris.

The impact of the design was so extraordinary that, it is said, police had to control the crowds of sightseers for two days after the building was officially opened. Not surprisingly, perhaps, this addition to the Bristol street scene raised hackles among the city's traditionalists. Stung by the criticism, Everard explained his ideas in a book – *A Bristol Printing House* – which, naturally, was printed by his own firm. It is now a collector's item.

The building was sensitively redeveloped by National Westminster Bank about twenty years ago, and now houses the group's insurance services. A small display in the entrance foyer contains items relating to the building.

Purists argue that, luxuriant though it is, this is a modified art nouveau design, lacking the sinuous tendril forms one associates with the full-blown extravaganzas of some European models. They suggest that, architecturally, the former Cabot Café on College Green, dating from 1904, is Bristol's premier example of genuine art nouveau.

If the current occupiers, the City's housing department, were ever to move, an authentically restored Edwardian tea house – emulating Mackintosh's Willow Tea Rooms in Glasgow – would be another gem in Bristol's architectural crown.

'Fairest, goodliest and most famous parish church ...'

Local guide-book writers should be eternally grateful to Queen Elizabeth I, even if there is no hard evidence that she did actually dub St Mary Redcliffe church 'the fairest, goodliest and most famous parish church in England'. Whether she uttered the immortal words on her visit in 1574 or not, the sentiment was echoed two centuries later by the boy poet Chatterton, who wrote that it was 'the pride of Brigstowe and the western land', and it has been endorsed by thousands of admiring visitors ever since.

St Mary Redcliffe is one of Bristol's treasures. No visitor to the city, however rushed, should leave without experiencing the wonder which this beautiful church always invokes. Its magnificent exterior, with flying buttresses, pinnacles and soaring spire, and its superb north porch, are matched by the splendour inside – slender columns soaring in uninterrupted majesty, 1200 roof bosses covered with gold, and its beautifully vaulted transepts, its great windows, fine Baroque ironwork and rare relics – relics, not of saints, it might be noted, but of Bristol's merchant venturers.

One of the greatest of these merchants, William Canynges the younger, lived in a splendid house on Redcliffe Backs, and was five times mayor of Bristol and its member of parliament twice. He owned the largest Bristol fleet in the fifteenth century, and put the wealth it created for him to good effect. He financed the restoration of the church, founded two chantries and after his wife's death, was ordained in 1468. A magnificent tomb shows the wealthy merchant and wife in splendid costume, while another effigy depicts Canynges the priest in more suitably simple dress.

Admiral Sir William Penn, born nearby in 1621, fought in the Dutch wars and was knighted for his naval exploits. He is buried at the entrance to the south transept, and his armour can be seen above an epitaph at the west end of the church. His son, also William, established a Quaker colony in America and gave his name to the state of Pennsylvania.

William Hogarth painted a great tryptych altarpiece for St Mary Redcliffe in 1755. The three panels, representing *The Ascension of Christ, The Sealing of the Sepulchre* and *The Three Marys at the Tomb*, fell victims to Victorian taste, were thrown out of the church nearly one hundred and fifty years ago, and after a chequered career are now seen to marvellous effect across the water in St Nicholas Church, where they adorn the tourist information centre. These paintings on the grand scale will surprise the visitor more familiar with Hogarth's satirical scenes of London low life. The artist's only other work on this scale were two large biblical paintings for St Bartholomew's Hospital in London in 1735.

Scholars now question the tradition that Handel played on the great new organ of St Mary Redcliffe, but the composer was a friend of Thomas Broughton, then vicar, and a Handel window, in which are scored eight passages from *The Messiah*, commemorates his links with the church. Thomas Chatterton passed much of his young life dreaming dreams amid the Gothic splendour and,

St Mary Redcliffe: the majestic north porch.

among other literary links, poets Coleridge and Southey were married to the Fricker sisters there in 1795.

St Mary Redcliffe's spectacular double-storeyed Early English north porch looks onto roaring traffic – a bleak setting for one of the country's finest churches. The long-term plan is to remove, or at least curb, the traffic and various proposals have been formulated to create a 'cathedral close' setting. The churchyard to the south, with its avenues of lime trees and backdrop of eighteenth-century houses in Colston Parade, is altogether more seemly. Its peace was shattered, though, in the 1941 blitz when a chunk of uprooted tramline was embedded in the graveyard, where it remains as a reminder of how close this great church itself came to disaster. Another curiosity is the memorial slab inscribed THE CHURCH CAT 1912-1927, who loved music and used to sit on the organist's knee while he was playing.

Nearby is Fry's House of Mercy, endowed by William Fry, a distiller, in 1784. Fry drew up the house rules. The almswomen, he decreed, should be well-bred, moral and religious; vicious persons and drunkards would not be admitted, and there would be a sixpenny fine for failure to attend church services. Number 9 Colston Parade was the birthplace of Samuel Plimsoll who campaigned for safety at sea.

Europe's Longest Crescent

Not as celebrated as Bath's Royal Crescent, perhaps – but certainly bigger! In fact, they reckon Royal York Crescent, dominating the Clifton skyline, is the longest crescent in Europe.

Like many of the grand Clifton set pieces, the crescent has had its ups and downs. Work started during the great speculative housing boom at the end of the eighteenth century, but this and other projects collapsed

Bristol's greatest crescent has unparalleled views across the city.

when war with France broke out in 1794. The partly completed crescent stood forlornly empty and unroofed until the last gaps were filled a quarter of a century later – but not before anxious Cliftonians had to fight off a threat that fifteen unfinished houses were to be converted into army barracks. The 'Nimby' culture is not, after all, a modern phenomenon.

When completed, the crescent became a local showpiece. Forty six houses provided spacious and elegant accommodation for residents and visitors. Each originally had a great drawing room on the first floor, measuring 23 feet wide, 28 feet deep and 13 feet high. Later conversion into flats has reduced the magnificence of the proportions, but these are still highly desirable places to live. Outside, a generous promenade stretches the length of the crescent with views across the city towards the Somerset hills.

Despite its grandeur, Royal York Crescent never achieved the cachet of Bath's famous crescent, which attracted so many of the great and not necessarily good that a book was written to chronicle the celebrities who have lived there down the years. But there were a few notable residents, including at Number 2 a little Spanish girl later to become Empress Eugenie of France, wife of Napoleon III. The house was then a fashionable school for young ladies.

Eugenie House, as it is now called, has a fine-traceried balcony – admiring the variety of the crescent's ironwork is one of the pleasures of a Sunday morning stroll along the flagstoned terrace.

Eugenie House – once school to a fledgling empress, now retirement homes.

Clifton

'Britain's leafiest suburb'

Sir John Betjeman was never happier than when visiting Clifton, immortalising its streets and churches in his celebrated verse. 'Bristol's biggest surprise is Clifton,' he also wrote, 'a sort of Bath consisting of Regency crescents and terraces overlooking the Avon Gorge to the blue hills of Somerset. The finest of them in size is Royal York Crescent ... and there are many handsome late-Georgian terraces ... Steep hills lead to steps: steps lead to terraces: and everywhere there are glimpses of gardens, delicate verandahs, lawns and trees. No English city has so large and leafy a suburb as Clifton. As the merchants climbed up the hill out of trade into the professions they moved to Clifton and from their Georgian houses went out to found the Empire ...'

Visitors have sung Clifton's praises for generations. Humphry Davy, later to be famed for his invention of the miner's safety lamp, wrote enthusiastically to his mother back in Cornwall in 1798: 'Clifton is situated on the top of a hill ... conveniently elevated above the dirt and noise of the city. Here are houses, rocks, woods, town and country in one small spot ... it almost rivals Penzance.' But not everyone was so impressed, for in the following year Lady Hesketh was complaining that 'the Bristol people have done all in their power to ruin the rural beauties of Clifton Hill by the number of abominable Buildings they have erected all over it'.

Clifton features in literature, not least in the gentle social satire of E.H. Young, in whose novels Upper Radstowe is a very thinly disguised decaying Clifton of the 1920s and 1930s. In *Miss Mole* (1930) she could write of how 'the

The Observatory on Clifton Down.

The stark lines of Clifton Cathedral.

houses in Upper Radstowe had a way of growing shabby and when Hannah stood at the gate peering in, she fancied that thus the ghosts of the eighteenth century

Simon Verity's font and William Haig's windows.

must stand and look at their fine houses going to decay, let out in flats, with the gathered perambulators and the bicycles of the inhabitants cumbering the stately entrance halls.'

The revival in Clifton's fortunes is now complete, and the most serious blots on its landscape as the century comes to an end are the proliferating commuters' cars and the threat of unwanted bars and 'themed' pubs.

Clifton, with its fine architecture and hidden nooks and crannies, breathtaking views, its cathedral, suspension bridge, zoo and rolling downs, and its artistic associations, needs a book to itself. And it has several, including Helen Reid's *Chronicle of Clifton and Hotwells*, as well as *Mostly Clifton*, with Cedric Barker's evocative photographs from the 1960s and 1970s.

No Laughing Matter

Humphry Davy came to Bristol in 1798 to help Dr Thomas Beddoes run the 'Pneumatic Institute' at Number 6 Dowry Square in Hotwells.   An advertisement in a Bristol newspaper explained that the institute was 'intended for the treatment of diseases hitherto found incurable.   The application of persons in confirmed consumption [tuberculosis] is principally wished at present.' There was a ready supply of invalids attracted to the supposed medicinal values of the local spa water.

Dowry Square had been developed in the early-eighteenth century to provide lodgings for visitors to the Hotwell spa, and many surgeons set up shop there. Beddoes was convinced, rightly, that air was more likely to help the tubercular than water – but was never quite able to persuade people that inhaling cows' breath was particularly healthy, even though one lady 'had her distressing symptoms all removed from living the winter in a room with four cows'.   Local landladies weighed in, complaining that they 'had not furnished their rooms for cattle'.

Meanwhile, Humphry Davy experimented with nitrous oxide, or laughing gas, often with truly hilarious results. Friends joined in, and managed to 'get high' by breathing the gas.   For Maria Edgeworth the gas 'inebriates in a most delightful manner', while Robert Southey commented that it made him laugh and tingle in toes and fingertips.   'Davy has invented a pleasure for which the language has no name.'

Beddoes' Pneumatic Institute saw strange experiments with gas.

Sadly, no one was cured of consumption, despite the wildest rumours about the nature of the experiments carried out there. But there was a lasting benefit: the gas that Davy's friends had such fun with has been used as an anaesthetic for toothache to this day.

Another of Dr Beddoes' assistants went on to achieve fame of an altogether different sort. After leaving Bristol, Peter Roget practised as a doctor in London and was senior secretary of The Royal Society for many years. But it wasn't until he was seventy – half a century after leaving Dowry Square – that he started on the ground-breaking *Thesaurus of English Words and Phrases* for which his name is still known today.

First for Fraud

Bristol can boast – if that's the word – one of the cleverest literary frauds of all time – Thomas Chatterton's medieval 'Rowley' poems which for a while fooled even the great Horace Walpole.

Chatterton was born within a stone's throw of St Mary Redcliffe church in 1752. He was the son of a charity school teacher and his modest birthplace survives, just off Redcliffe Way. The young poet's father had died by the time Thomas was born and a culturally deprived background, frustrated ambition and a soaring romanticism inspired by the Gothic splendour and antiquities of the nearby church, combined to produce one of English literature's most bizarre episodes.

Chatterton had achieved a modest literary success before he was into his teens, when a local newspaper published some of his satirical verse. But there was no one to channel his precocious talents. Instead, the young lad spent many hours in the muniment room over the north porch at St Mary Redcliffe, studying old manuscripts which were quite clearly the inspiration and model for his flawed literary efforts. Leaving Colston School, where he found the commercial emphasis stifling, he became articled to John Lambert, an attorney with offices in Corn Street. Bored with this drudgery, he began to fashion the mock medieval poems which he attributed to Thomas Rowley, a fictitious fifteenth-century priest.

The Rowley poems were well enough done to fool the public initially and the controversy about their authenticity rumbled on after the young poet's death. In 1776

St Mary Redcliffe as Chatterton would have known it: water-colour drawing by T.L.S. Rowbotham.

Samuel Johnson, accompanied by the faithful Boswell, was persuaded to make a special visit to the muniment room. By then the 'marvellous boy, the sleepless soul that perished in his pride', in Wordsworth's lines, had been dead for six years. Johnson, not fooled, nevertheless commented: 'This is the most extraordinary young man that has encountered my knowledge. It is wonderful how the whelp has written such things.'

Chatterton was sacked when his Corn Street employer discovered a maliciously worded 'will'. He left for London, embittered by his lack of true recognition, worked furiously for a while but finally committed suicide in a Holborn garret in August, 1770. He was seventeen years old. A famous Victorian portrayal of the deathbed scene, *The Death of Chatterton*, by Henry Wallis is in the Tate Gallery. The Chatterton tragedy clearly appealed to Victorian sentiment, as Henrietta Ward's painting of the young Chatterton at home with his family was a popular exhibit at the Royal Academy in 1873. It is now to be found in Bristol City Art Gallery.

Chatterton's parting sally suggests he wasn't entirely unhappy to leave Bristol:

> Farewell, Bristolia's dingy pile of brick,
> Lovers of Mammon, worshippers of Trick!
> ... Farewell, ye guzzling aldermanic fools,
> By nature fitted for Corruption's tools!

To young poets, Chatterton became a cult figure and an inspiration to the burgeoning Romantic Movement. His death inspired novels, a play by Alfred de Vigny, an opera, and biographies. Coleridge wrote his 'Monody on the Death of Chatterton', while Keats composed a sonnet to his memory and dedicated 'Endymion' to him. In our own time, the Chatterton story has inspired a masterly novel by Peter Ackroyd.

The quality of his astonishing output – by no means limited to the forgeries and in print running to over 600 pages – was uneven but remarkably mature for someone so young. Much of it can be read with real pleasure today.

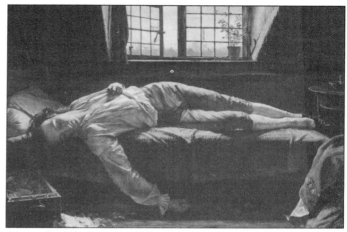

Henry Wallis: Death of Chatterton.

Bristol and the Romantic Movement

It's maybe fanciful to suggest that a handshake changed the face of English poetry. But a meeting in Bristol certainly played a pivotal role in the early years of what came to be known as the Romantic Movement. The names of William Wordsworth and Samuel Taylor Coleridge are inextricably linked with John Pinney's house at 7 Great George Street, where Wordsworth stayed in the 1790s, although there is some doubt as to whether this is where the two poets first met. Many years later, Wordsworth recalled that he had first met Coleridge and Robert Southey in a Bristol lodging house, and another version has it that they sought each other out at a political debate.

Whatever the accident of that first meeting, it was to lead to the momentous first publication of *Lyrical Ballads* in a Bristol bookseller's parlour. Joseph Cottle had known and generously published Coleridge and Southey for some years, but his great claim to fame was to be the slim volume which included Coleridge's 'The Rime of the Ancient Mariner' and Wordsworth's 'Tintern Abbey'. Wordsworth was still putting the finishing touches to this, his first great poem, as he and sister Dorothy strode down Park Street, having walked across the Downs from the Severn ferry at Aust. Weeks later, in September, 1798, the famous book first saw the light of day.

Coleridge had wanted anonymity from the outset, pleading that 'Wordsworth's name is nothing to a large number of people; mine stinks' and the initial disappointing reception to the 500-copy edition seemed to justify his reticence. Wordsworth, too, had mixed feel-ings about publication. When Cottle, beset by financial problems, prevaricated Wordsworth thought of going elsewhere, but was also saying that 'it [publication] is a thing which I dread as much as death itself'.

Cottle disposed of the unsold copies to a London book-seller, and the rights to Longman. Although, for him, it was a financial failure, *Lyrical Ballads* was the crowning point of an intense period of literary activity centred on his premises in High Street and later, before bankruptcy engulfed him, at 5 Wine Street. Cottle published early work by Coleridge, and financed his periodical, *The Watchman*; he also published Southey and Charles Lamb,

Georgian elegance recreated at The Georgian House.

Samuel Taylor Coleridge: his meeting with Wordsworth was a turning point in English literature.

and, when his fortunes had improved, brought out a definitive edition of the works of Thomas Chatterton. Great patron and judge of poetry though he was, the least said of his own literary efforts the better.

The Georgian House, as 7 Great George Street is now known, is a fine town house built in 1791 by the noted Bristol architect, William Paty. Apart from Pinney's literary circle, eminent visitors are believed to include Lord Nelson. The last private owner, Canon Cole was a prominent local antiquarian who donated the house to the Corporation in 1938 to display Georgian furniture and other domestic fittings. It opened the following year as the first museum of its kind in England to be set in an actual Georgian house. Visitors can explore eighteenth-century life upstairs and down, from elegantly furnished reception rooms with delicate plasterwork to the basement kitchen, complete with roasting spit, oven and pots and pans. Most of the period furniture was introduced, but one of the finest pieces is the built-in bookcase which was originally in John Pinney's office.

The Georgian House is open: Apr 1-Oct 31 Sat-Wed, 10am-5pm. Admission charge (except for leisure card-holders, children under 16 and full time students).

Domestic life from yesteryear is also recalled in Blaise Castle House, at Henbury, another fine late-eighteenth century house. Once the home of the Harford family, who employed Humphry Repton to landscape their gardens, the museum is full of children's toys, mangles and washtubs, and elegant Victorian gowns. Open: Apr 1-Oct 31 Sat-Wed, 10am-5pm. Admission free.

First Heard in Bristol

At least three everyday sayings can be traced back to a Bristol origin. **'Ship-shape and Bristol fashion'**, commonly used to mean neat and tidy, originally had a more specific meaning. Before the present floating harbour was built, the Avon river was tidal right up to the centre of the city, and the difference in water level between ebb and flood was something like thirty feet. This exceptionally high rise and fall of the tide meant that ships were often left stranded on mudbanks. At low tide, ships in harbour, if not properly constructed – 'ship-shape and Bristol fashion' – could break their backs and their cargoes could shift perilously.

Stand around the top end of Corn Street, and, sooner or later, you'll hear a Bristol resident explaining the origin of the expression **'paying on the nail'**. The four flat-topped bronze pillars, or nails, outside the Exchange have given rise to one of Bristol's many pieces of harmless mythology. Originally situated on the north side of All Saints' church in a covered walk called the Tolzey, they were moved the short distance to their present site in 1771.

For many years, the nails were used by merchants to show their samples and strike bargains. The edges are raised, originally to stop the coins rolling off into the mud. Bristol's claim to originate the saying, though, is a fragile one. Much simpler 'nails', driven into the bare earth, were commonly seen in medieval fairs, and Bath has pillars similar to Bristol's.

The delightful phrase **'happy as a sandboy'** originated, it is said, in an ancient Bristol inn. The Ostrich is on the waterfront, just round the corner from Redcliffe caves which were once an important source of sand for glass-making and other local industries. Landlords at the inn would send young lads to collect sand from the caves to spread on the floor to soak up the spilt beer. Who wouldn't be happy as a sandboy to be given free beer for a relatively modest chore like that?

The labyrinthine Redcliffe caves extend for hundreds of yards below the surrounding streets and buildings. They are opened periodically, when they attract thousands of curious visitors.

'Paying on the nail', Bristol fashion.

Bristol's Changing Time

How many people crossing Bristol Bridge have noticed something odd about St Nicholas church in Baldwin Street? Closer inspection of the clock face will show it has three hands. This is generally reckoned to be the only public clock in the country to have a second hand. For a period, though, it didn't: its mechanism was destroyed in the war, and then replaced in 1960.

Just round the corner, in Corn Street, is yet another clock with three hands. But the extra hand on the Exchange clock isn't meant for the punctilious time-watcher. This time-piece has two minute hands – that in red showing original 'Bristol' time: a reminder of the years when Bristol, 120 miles west of London, was literally ten minutes behind the capital. The extra hand was reinstated in 1989 as a historical curiosity.

It's easy in these days of instant global communication to forget that Britain's time wasn't standardised until the coming of the telegraphic service and the railways. The railways ran to Greenwich mean time, and Bristol Corporation thoughtfully added the extra hand to the Exchange clock, so that there was one minute hand for local time and one for the railway traveller. Eventually, the growing use of telegrams provided the coup de grace. People found it incongruous to receive a message apparently before it had been sent, and the Bristol council, along with others outside the capital city, voted to put their local time forward.

The Palladian-fronted Exchange itself, completed in

The Exchange clock shows Bristol ten minutes behind Greenwich mean time.

1743, is one of Bristol finest buildings and, as architectural historian Timothy Mowl has pointed out, it was then the city's most ambitious building since St Mary Redcliffe church in the Middle Ages. It was built around an open court, exposed to the elements, and in time merchants were to switch their allegiance to the greater comfort of Busby's nearby Commercial Rooms when they were built in 1811. Things improved when part of the Exchange was allocated to corn merchants and, eventually, the open area was roofed over. Despite its situation in Corn Street, the Exchange had in fact been built for general business use and not originally for the corn trade.

The Exchange was designed by the noted architect, John Wood of Bath, who was self-evidently pleased with his own work, for he described the finished building in verse as:

> ... A stately Pile by publick Spirit plann'd
> Politely finished – regularly Grand
> With striking Beauties how it charms our Eyes!

.... concluding, correctly as it happens, that 'this spacious Dome' would be 'A finish'd Wonder for each Age to come'.

A few yards from the Exchange, another time-piece entertains the visitor. Christ Church, at the meeting of Corn Street, Broad Street and Wine Street, boasts a pair of wooden quarter-jacks. These colourful figures, in Roman dress, strike their bells each quarter hour. They were carved in 1728 by Thomas Paty, a member of a local family of craftsmen whose work is to be seen in and on buildings throughout the city.

The quarter-jacks at Christ Church.

David Garrick's Finest Theatre in Europe

King Street, just off the city centre, has a wonderful variety of interesting buildings, from ancient almshouses to half-timbered inns. The grandest is the eighteenth-century Theatre Royal, the oldest working theatre in the country.

David Garrick, the celebrated actor, strangely never performed here, but he wrote the prologue to Steel's *The Conscious Lovers* with which the theatre opened in 1766, and described it as the most beautiful theatre in Europe. The opening night had to be advertised as 'a concert of music interspersed with specimens of rhetorick'. The Puritans had failed to prevent the theatre being built but, at least initially, had succeeded in denying it a licence to perform plays.

When it first opened, the Theatre Royal catered for the wealthy merchants living in King Street and nearby Queen Square. It flourished for many years, but competition and the social decline of the docks area around King Street saw its fortunes slide. At one stage the city's finest theatre was reduced to performing third rate variety acts to audiences who would have horrified the leaders of local society who flocked there in its golden days. By the early 1940s, the theatre was on the verge of being turned into a fruit and vegetable warehouse, when it was acquired by public-spirited citizens and leased to the forerunner of the Arts Council, which sponsored its wartime productions.

After the war, the Bristol Old Vic Company was established and, two hundred years after the theatre first opened, an ambitious restoration scheme embraced the adjoining Palladian Coopers' Hall which now provides the magnificent frontage and entrance which greets today's theatre-goers.

An almost endless roll call of eminent performers have trod the Theatre Royal boards. The greatest tragic actress on the British stage, Sarah Siddons shuttled between the Bath and Bristol theatres, and was known to give a major performance in two theatres on the same day. She much preferred the West Country to London, and made quite a family thing of it, sometimes bringing

Sarah Siddons: the darling of Bristol theatre-goers.

Britain's oldest working theatre.

her children onto the King Street stage for a curtain speech. Some say her ghost still haunts the theatre.

A scintillating cast list of actors and actresses contributed their memories of playing to Bristol audiences in the fund-raising book, *Not in the Script*, which can be bought at the theatre.

A few yards west of the Theatre Royal is the imposing Old Library – now a restaurant – which was built in 1739 on the site of the first public lending library to open in Bristol, and indeed one of the first anywhere in the country. The names of Coleridge and Wordsworth are to be found among the old records. When the present central library opened, the best feature among the fittings to accompany the books across College Green was the beautiful overmantel, probably by Grinling Gibbons. This masterly riot of carved flowers, fruit and game birds can now be seen in the library's Bristol Room.

First for Smooth Roads

Road builders haven't always enjoyed a bad press. Back in 1815, John Loudon McAdam was appointed Surveyor to the Bristol Turnpike Trust, and was soon giving Bristol some of the best roads in the country. The new, improved roads were built up with layers of broken stones, crushed into position by traffic or heavy roller. According to the Oxford English Dictionary, the verb 'to macadamize' was first used in 1825.

A plaque at 23 Berkeley Square records that McAdam lived there from 1805 to 1808. In 1815, he was living at 6 Sion Hill, Clifton, and died in 1836 at the age of eighty.

A Scot who came to live in Bristol in 1801, McAdam was the first president of the Bristol Commercial Coffee Rooms, which was to play a leading part in the city's business life. At one stage there were more than one thousand members until, like so many gentlemen's clubs, it succumbed to changing social patterns and falling membership. The Rooms, in Corn Street, were designed by C.A. Busby in 1811 and contain some notable architectural features, including a lovely lantern light with twelve caryatids holding the saucer dome. An elegant wind vane, still in working order, served originally to show whether the wind was favourable for ships to sail up the Avon.

Once enjoyed only by Bristol merchants, all this can now be seen by the general public, as the building has been converted into a public house. Unlike most pub conversions, which are usually crassly done, this one has been carried out in an exemplary manner, earning a coveted English Heritage conservation award. Outside, the Grecian exterior is topped by three statues representing the city, commerce and navigation, and the relief over the portico represents Britannia, with Neptune and Minerva, receiving tributes from the far corners of the earth.

First Mail Coach Left From Bristol

History was in the making as the mail coach rumbled away from the Rummer Inn at four o'clock on the afternoon of Monday 2 August, 1784, heading for Bath and the Great West Road en route to London. This first mail run arrived at the Swan with Two Necks, in Lad Lane, London 'well before eight o'clock' the following morning. The cost of sending a letter to London by the new system was a far from paltry sixpence – but it was a lot cheaper than the laborious, slow and risky system of postboys, which took two days and cost two shillings for a letter.

The new system was the brain-child of theatre lessee John Palmer, who ran the two Theatre Royals in Bristol and Bath. During the course of his work as manager, Palmer travelled extensively looking for fresh theatrical talent and gained a detailed knowledge of transport around the country. He was less than impressed by what he saw of the postal service: 'the Mail is generally entrusted to some idle boy without character, mounted on a worn out hack who so far from being able to defend himself or escape from a robber is more likely to be in league with him.'

In 1782, Palmer devoted himself to the reform of the postal delivery system. An introduction to Prime Minister William Pitt enabled him to outline his proposal for armed coaches instead of post-boys on horseback. Despite stiff opposition from the Post Office, who put every possible objection in the way of reform, Palmer eventually had his way, and Bristol was chosen for the experimental run. Within days, the press were reporting that 'the excellent steps taken to carry out this undertaking leave not the least room to doubt of its succeeding to the great pleasure and advantage of the public.'

For sixpence one could now post a letter in Bristol at 3.30pm on Monday and the letter could be collected at the London GPO on Tuesday morning. A reply written the same day and posted by 7.30pm in Lombard Street could be collected before noon on Wednesday from the Post Office in Small Street in Bristol – an astonishing service for the time. Postage was paid by the person receiving the letter.

Palmer still had his enemies in the postal service, who complained about the extra costs involved. For a time, he was forced to run the mail service at his own expense. Although the Post Office die-hards eventually managed to engineer his dismissal, Palmer triumphed in the end and was granted a handsome pension for his pains.

By the early 1830s, the journey time had been further reduced, with the Bristol Mail leaving London at 8 o'clock in the evening and arriving at the Bush Inn, Corn Street at nine the following morning. Little more could be achieved by horse-power and, a decade later, the mail train had slashed the journey to just over four hours.

The mail is rushed from Bristol to London.

Queen Square

Largest of them all?

The houses themselves might not be particularly distinguished, but Queen Square is certainly an impressive open space to find in the heart of a great provincial city. An immense square, it is the country's largest outside Lincoln's Inn Fields in London – and some claim it is larger even than that. Whatever, Queen Square has a history to match its size – and several 'firsts' to its name. An early example of town planning, it was built at the start of the eighteenth century – on a public marsh outside the original city which was once used for bull baiting – in an attempt to rival the grand new developments in London and to flag the city fathers' modern outlook, red brick frontages and all.

For Alexander Pope, writing of Bristol in 1739, the Square was a redeeming feature. 'The streets are as crowded as London but the best Image I can give you of it is 'Tis as if Wapping and Southwark were ten-times as big, or all their people run into London. Nothing is fine in it but the square, which is larger than Grosvenor-Square and wellbuilded ... And the Key which is full of ships and goes half round this square.' This was the Age of Reason, of course, and it is easy to see why Pope preferred the order of Queen Square to the riot of Bristol's medieval streets.

The central grounds were laid out as a formal garden with gravel paths. Rysbrack's statue of William III, dressed as a Roman emperor and seated on a noble beast, was commissioned by a prestige-conscious city council and erected in 1736. Who is to dispute that this is Britain's finest equestrian statue? The whole ensemble –

'state of the art' houses, promenades, trees and sophisticated sculpture – presented a sedate contrast to the cramped, malodorous and still largely timber-built medieval city and its bustling waterfront. Its social life centred on the nearby Theatre Royal in King Street and the now-demolished Assembly Rooms in Prince Street.

Queen Square was the scene of the infamous Bristol Riots of 1831, when drunken mobs plundered and burnt down the Mansion House and Customs House and with them all the north side and most of the west side of the square. The troubles were sparked by the great Reform issue but also reflected the deep social divisions of the time. Unrest came to a head when Sir Charles Wetherell, the deeply unliked Recorder of Bristol, came to open the assizes. Wetherell was a staunch opponent of parliamentary reform, trouble was expected and Government troops were drafted in to help keep the peace. The mere presence of the cavalry made things worse. Wetherell succeeded in opening the assizes at the Guildhall and reached the Mansion House in Queen Square, shaken but unharmed, before fleeing the city in disguise. The riots now started in earnest. The Mansion House was looted and destroyed, the Customs House and private houses in the square suffering the same fate; drunken looters roamed the streets, the gaols were burned and their prisoners released, and the Bishop's Palace was destroyed. The riots lasted three days until troop reinforcements finally restored law and order.

William Muller has left us a lurid pictorial record of those three days of madness, but the most vivid account was

Early town planning: Queen Square before the Bristol Riots of 1831.

given by writer Charles Kingsley. He was then a schoolboy in Bristol and later in life recalled that 'the fog hung thick over the docks and lowlands. Glaring through the fog I saw a bright mass of flame, almost like a half-risen sun. That, I was told, was the gate of the new gaol on fire ... By ten o'clock that night one seemed to be looking down upon Dante's Inferno, and to hear the multitudinous moan and wail of lost spirits surging to and fro amid that sea of fire ... miles away, I could see the lovely tower of Dundry shining red – the symbol of the old faith, looking down in stately wonder and sorrow upon the fearful birth-throes of a new age.'

William III: Britain's finest equestrian statue?

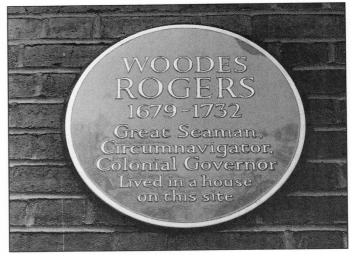

Woodes Rogers was a noted resident.

Although fewer than one third of its original buildings have survived, Queen Square remains a handsome show piece. An early resident at number 35 was Captain Woodes Rogers whose popular claim to fame was his friendship with Alexander Selkirk upon whose exploits Defoe based *Robinson Crusoe*. A plaque describes him as a 'Great Seaman, Circumnavigator and Colonial Governor'. Nearby Number 37 housed the first American consulate in Britain and a plaque tells us that Kosciuszko, the Polish patriot, stayed here in 1797. Eça de Quieroz, the great Portuguese writer, was his country's consul at Number 33 from 1878 to 1888. He wrote part of his *Letters from England* while working there and living at 38 Stoke Hill.

Although still badly disfigured by cars parked on office forecourts, the square has been partly relieved of the curse of polluting traffic, and there are plans to dig up the road which for more than half a century has slashed diagonally across the green. When traffic is totally banned from the perimeter road, Queen Square will once again be a haven of quiet in the busy city.

First for Charity

Near the Cenotaph on the city centre stands the statue of an outstanding benefactor in a city famed for its charitable institutions. Edward Colston made most of his fortune in London, but it was his birthplace in 1636 which received most of his charity – to the tune, probably, of around £100,000, then a vast sum of money. His good works are to be seen throughout the city – two schools, the great almshouses on St Michael's Hill, improvements to almshouses in King Street, as well as restoration work on the cathedral and other churches. But his influence extends beyond his personal benefactions, for the charitable societies founded after his death still flourish.

The city's bells tolled for sixteen hours when Colston's body was brought back to Bristol on his death at Mortlake in 1721. He lies in All Saints' church, City, marked by a statue by Rysbrack. The statue on the centre was erected in 1895. Its designer, John Cassidy, depicted the philanthropist leaning thoughtfully on his staff musing, perhaps, on his involvement with the slave trade.

Edward Colston ponders the morality of the slave trade.

Bristol in the 1820s

Thanks to Mr Braikenridge

It's easy to take Bristol's treasures for granted – like the incomparable collection of early nineteenth-century drawings and watercolours of the city in the decades before the camera was available to do the job. And that unique picture they give of Bristol streets and buildings before the Victorian 'improvers' got to work was the inspiration of one man – the antiquarian George Weare Braikenridge, retired merchant and West Indies plantation owner who commissioned nearly 1500 drawings and watercolours of Bristol in the 1820s. It is an invaluable archive for historians and architects. No other city has such an extensive and detailed record of how it looked in the early years of the last century.

Work by the Braikenridge artists is always on display at the City Art Gallery, and other examples can be seen on request. Pictures from the collection are frequently used to illustrate local history studies. About fifty were published in *The Bristol Scene*, a small book which reproduces local scenes by Francis Danby, Samuel Jackson, T.L.S. Rowbotham and others.

Some of the artists, like Samuel Jackson, are well known in their own right and have a substantial body of work to their name, but others, like Rowbotham, are more or less unknown outside the collection.

The Braikenridge pictures are just part of the city's fine collection of paintings by artists of the Bristol School, as well as other important British art of the nineteenth and twentieth centuries. Work can also be seen by Italian and North European artists of the fifteenth to eighteenth

Rowbotham drawing of Corn Street in 1825. The Bush on the left was a celebrated coaching inn; the two churches – Christ Church and All Saints' – remain, as does the Exchange behind the railings.

centuries and by the impressionists and other nineteenth-century French artists.

The impressive applied art galleries include wonderful displays of local glass, ceramics and furniture. Bristol can claim the largest collection of English delftware in the world. There is an internationally important collection of Oriental art, including superb examples of Chinese ceramics and Japanese prints, as well as Islamic carpets, textiles and costume – all among the finest to be seen in western Europe. There is plenty to see throughout the museum – the colour and fire of the mineral collection, the mysteries of ancient Egypt, the long extinct 'sea dragons', along with native and overseas birds and mammals.

Open: daily, 10am-5pm. Closed some bank holidays. Admission charge (except for leisure card-holders, children under 16 and full time students who enjoy free admission to all museums run by Bristol City Council).

Tinglazed earthenware bowl, 1755, probably manufactured in Bristol.

Shop and restaurant.

A few hundred yards along Queen's Road from the City Art Gallery, the **Royal West of England Academy** holds its annual show of members' work each November, and a varied programme of exhibitions throughout the year. Housed in an imposing Italianate pile, the RWA is one of Bristol's great institutions. It was founded in the mid-nineteenth century with financial backing by Ellen, the mother of artist Rolinda Sharples who is remembered today for her intriguing scenes of Bristol social life.

Open: Mon-Sat 10am-5.30pm; Sundays 2-5pm. Admission charge to exhibitions, but free admission to shop.

Self portrait by Rolinda Sharples.

Arnolfini: interior.

Arnolfini: one of the country's finest venues for contemporary art.

At the other end of the spectrum, **Arnolfini** on Narrow Quay is a nationally-known venue for the contemporary arts, with galleries in the converted Bush Warehouse, once used for the import of tea. It is also a venue for cinema, contemporary dance and performance, and has a shop and waterside restaurant specialising in fish and vegetarian dishes. Arnolfini had three temporary homes during the 1960s and early-'70s; the Bush House conversion in 1975 not only gave them space to breath, but was a trail-blazing example of how redundant dockside buildings could be put to new use.

Open: Mon-Sat, 10am-11pm, Sunday 12 noon-10.30pm.

Across St Augustine's Reach, **Watershed** was another trail-blazer when it opened in 1984 as the first media centre of its kind in the country. The centre includes cinema, photography exhibitions and public access to photographic dark rooms using the most up-to-date digital technology. Watershed is one of the venues for the Wildscreen festival of wildlife film and television. Its café overlooking the water is a popular meeting place. Open daily.

World's Highest Cricket Score

Thirteen years is a tender age at which to set a world cricketing record – one that has now lasted almost one hundred years. And yet A.E.J. Collins was still two months short of his fourteenth birthday when he stepped from obscurity onto the Clifton College Close to score a breath-taking 628 runs in a junior house match in June 1899.

In a corner of the Clifton College Close, A.E.J. Collins made his record-breaking cricket score.

This really was *Boys' Own* stuff in the days when cricket was still taken seriously at school, and achievement on the playing field was seen as a metaphor for the bigger struggles to come in later life.

Only two years earlier, Old Cliftonian Henry Newbolt had published his stirring 'Vitai Lampada', with the lines generations of school children would come to learn by heart:

> There's a breathless hush in the Close to-night –
>   Ten to make and the match to win –
> A bumping pitch and a blinding light,
>   An hour to play and the last man in.
> And it's not for the sake of a ribboned coat,
>   Or the selfish hope of a season's fame,
> But his Captain's hand on his shoulder smote –
>   'Play up! Play up! and play the game!'

A.E.J. Collins was captaining Clark's House against North Town's Junior XI, and winning the toss, elected to bat. Opening the batting, he had scored 200 runs by the end of the first afternoon. His score had risen to 509 when stumps were drawn the following afternoon. By then he had passed the record of 485 set by the Middlesex batsman, A.E. Stoddart playing in a club match in Hampstead in 1886. As word spread through the city, crowds flocked to Guthrie Road on the third day, when only fifty-five minutes were played but which saw the young prodigy take his score to 598.

Clark's House were finally all out for 836, with Collins carrying his bat for 628 'plus or minus 20, shall we say', according to the schoolboy scorer. Overwhelmed, their opponents were then bowled out twice for a total of 148. The bowler who took eleven of their wickets was none other than A.E.J. Collins!

Just how great an achievement was it? The opposition was not all that weak – four went on to play for the school First XI. Two sides of the ground were very short – but as boundaries, reflecting this, counted only two runs, some observers said the hard-hitting Collins would have scored many more runs on a bigger ground (his 146 boundaries alone could have been worth 584 if they had counted for the more usual four runs). And although he was dropped four times, this was not until his score had reached first 400 and then 566, 605 and 619, by which time all involved – batsman, bowlers and fielders – were doubtless flagging.

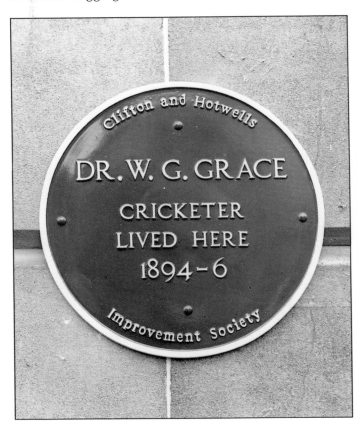

'W.G.' graced this corner of Victoria Square.

In reality this was a freak score by a good, but not exceptionally outstanding, cricketer. A fine all-round sportsman, Collins went on to score well for the school and in club cricket. But nothing he did in later life could match the exploits of those halcyon afternoons that late-Victorian summer. He died in the Great War at the age of twenty-eight.

The Clifton College cricket fields were a happy hunting ground for others. Thirty or so years before Collins' innings Edward Tylecote, another college boy, had struck a remarkable 404 not out. And W.G. Grace, probably the most famous cricketer of them all, scored 13 of his 126 first-class hundreds on the Close, in the days when Gloucestershire played in Clifton during the school holidays – making this his favourite ground after Lord's and The Oval.

A wall plaque in Guthrie Road, Clifton marks the young Collins' singular achievement, while 'W.G.'s residence at Number 16 Victoria Square from 1894 to 1896 is similarly recorded.

First for Wildlife

Bristol Zoo, between Clifton College and Durdham Downs, is the fifth oldest zoo in the world and has been open to the public longer than any other zoo in the country. It is home to over 300 species of wildlife. The gardens have been a popular feature since the zoo was created in 1834 by 225 Bristolians each subscribing £25, and are periodically the venue for open-air Shakespearean productions and other events.

Bristol is in the forefront of enlightened zoo management, with a strong emphasis on conservation and education, a popular 'hands-on' activity centre, an interactive Zoolympics trail, bird displays and feeding time talks.

Open: daily 9.30am-5.30pm (4.30pm in winter), except for Christmas Day. Admission charge.

Wildscreen, another great Bristol success story, is the world's biggest festival of wildlife film and television. The biennial festival was first held in 1982, and in 1996 attracted a record 327 entries from 36 different countries. It is staged at a number of venues around the inner harbour, including Watershed Media Centre, Arnolfini and the Leadworks.

The coveted Panda Awards are recognised as the top natural history awards in the industry, reflecting the Festival's close association with the World Wildlife Fund. Free screenings of the best entries are held at Watershed during the festival, when 5000 tickets are given to schools and the general public.

The coveted 'Panda' award for wildlife film.

The Red Lodge

Pilot Girls' Reformatory School

The Red Lodge, on Park Row, is firmly on any visitor's 'must see' list. Behind a plain red door at the top of a steep street behind the Colston Hall lies one of Bristol's greatest treasures – a lavish Elizabethan interior. Its superb Great Oak Room, hardly changed in four hundred years, has intricately carved panelling, a magnificent interior porch, plasterwork and – the crowning feature – an elaborately carved stone chimney piece. This is the only Bristol fireplace of its period still *in situ*, although another fine example, removed from a house in Lewin's Mead, may be seen in Danby's Restaurant at the City Museum & Art Gallery. There are other fine rooms and furniture throughout Red Lodge.

A courtyard garden contains a copy of an Elizabethan knot garden of box hedges in a pattern taken from the Lodge's bedroom ceiling. Most of the plants would have been familiar to the original residents.

The Red Lodge was built for John Yonge in 1590 as one of two lodges to his Great House where Queen Elizabeth stayed on her visit to Bristol in 1574 and may, or may not, have marvelled at the beauty of St Mary Redcliffe church.

In 1854, Mary Carpenter, with financial help from Lady Byron, the poet's widow, used the Red Lodge as the first girls' reformatory school in the country – 'for the restoration to society of girls who have cut themselves off by dishonest practices' – and remained in charge until her death twenty-three years later. She had previously opened a ragged school in 1846 and knew all about deprived children. At the Red Lodge, she worked heroically in the face of riots, absconding girls, pregnancies and arson, and won through. Many of her charges came out reformed to lead normal lives.

She also travelled, making several trips to India, and wrote and campaigned for women's education. She died in 1877, a national figure. The school eventually closed in 1919, and a small room is now devoted to a display of the reformer's life and work.

Mary Carpenter had started as a social worker by opening a single room in Lewin's Mead, and later established a reformatory school in a Kingswood house once

The splendid Elizabethan interior at the Red Lodge.

A box-hedge knot garden in the centre of a great city.

used by John Wesley – before devoting herself to the exclusive care of wayward girls. As well as the Red Lodge plaque, a bust in Bristol Cathedral celebrates her selfless life.

Among earlier occupants was James Cowles Prichard, a physician at Bristol Royal Infirmary who lived here with his family from 1827. He researched and wrote *The Natural History of Man* while living at the Red Lodge, and many of his ideas pre-dated those of Charles Darwin.

The Red Lodge is also noted as the home of Bristol Savages, a group of Bristol artists who have their 'wigwam' in an extension to the main building. The club was founded in 1894, originally for artists only, but the membership was later extended. There are now three classes of members: artists, who wear a red feather, blue feather entertainers and 'lay' members who sport the green. Members meet once a week, when the focus is the traditional two-hour sketch, when the artists have to depict a subject nominated by their chairman for the evening. The evening's entertainment consists of poetry readings, monologues, song, piano and instrumental music.

Early members included Wilde Parsons, Ernest Board, who painted immense tableaux of Bristol events, and Bartram Hiles, who lost both arms in a childhood accident but trained himself to hold a brush in his teeth – well enough to have a painting exhibited at the Royal Academy in 1909.

Leading lights in the Savages were instrumental in saving and restoring the Red Lodge and its prized furnishings when the reformatory closed. In the philistine 1920s, which saw many fine buildings broken up, there was a very real threat it might be demolished. After this period of stewardship, the building passed into the ownership of the City Council in 1948 and is now open to the public: Apr 1-October 31 Sat-Wed, 10am-5pm. Admission charge (except for leisure card-holders, children under 16 and full time students).

Three Men in a Bristol Cellar

Jerome K. Jerome's timeless classic *Three Men in a Boat* and George Grossmith's *Diary of a Nobody* were just two best-selling Victorian classics which first saw the murky light of day in a printer's cellar in Bristol. Quay Street, when ships still moored well into Bristol's Centre, was the home of printers, J.W. Arrowsmith, once famed as publishers of railway timetables.

In 1883, Arrowsmith's attempts to break into general publishing bore spectacular fruits when he persuaded an estate agent chum, Fred Fargus to pen a 'shilling shocker' for him. *Called Back*, published under the pseudonym 'Hugh Conway' proved an unlikely success and led to a spate of contracts with popular writers of the day – from Marie Corelli to Anthony Hope and Conan Doyle.

Humorist Jerome K. Jerome was no fool when it came to business, as his correspondence with Arrowsmith showed. He had already notched up impressive sales with light-hearted 'middlebrow' fare like *Idle Thoughts of an Idle Fellow*, and was far from being a budding writer. He wrote to the Bristol firm in February, 1889 offering his comic tale of a trip up the Thames. A few months' haggling over terms and illustrations followed, in which a confident Jerome talked the publisher up from a retail price of one shilling to 3/6d as 'this is the price I know I can get from a London house'. Jerome was clearly anxious to be published by Arrowsmiths, which he considered 'for energy and push, I suppose clearly the leading firm'.

So *Three Men in a Boat* appeared on the bookstalls in September, 1889 – to howls of abuse from the reviewers

The young Jerome K. Jerome who wanted to be published in Bristol.

and howls of laughter from the public. The serious press were outraged by the vulgarity of the humour and the colloquial writing style. The staidly satirical magazine *Punch*, Jerome later recalled, 'was especially indignant ... One might have imagined – to read some of the critics – that the British Empire was in danger.'

Jerome's comic masterpiece was soon reducing readers to hysterical laughter all over the world. In South Africa, it appeared as *Dri Swape op De Rivier*; its Portuguese publisher gave it the title *Tres Inglises No Estrangeiro*, while the Russian edition outsold all other translations except the German. Jerome did well out of the book, but did not become absurdly rich. Many of the overseas editions were 'pirated', and the author did not receive a single penny from sales of over one million copies in America.

Three Men in a Boat is almost as popular today as it was when Arrowsmith simply couldn't get copies out of Bristol and onto the bookstands quickly enough. It has sold over three million copies in its English editions alone. It has become a Penguin classic, been filmed three times and dramatised by Tom Stoppard.

But much of this has happened long after Arrowsmiths pulled out of general publishing. After those phenomenal early successes, the golden touch eluded the firm as the twentieth century wore on, and it quietly dropped literature to concentrate on commercial printing.

From Boxkite to Concorde

Just inside the entrance to the City Museum in Queen's Road hangs a fragile-looking reminder of the Bristol exploits of 'those daring young men in their flying machines' – a replica of the cotton, wood and piano wire-Boxkite biplane which, back in 1910, helped pioneer Britain's emerging aviation industry.

The business genius behind those early experimental and show flights over Clifton Downs and the Avon Gorge was Sir George White, the entrepreneur extraordinaire who had already given Bristol the country's first electric tramway service. Sir George was no dabbler in fanciful 'might work' schemes: his shrewd brain weighed the business risk, and he usually got it right. He set up his British & Colonial Aeroplane Company, with associated enterprises, in 1910. Only two other British aeroplane companies of any note – Short Brothers and Handley Page – had got off the ground, and George White's enterprise was more strongly capitalised than theirs; the Filton plant was the first large-scale site for aeroplane production in Britain, and by 1911 was claimed to be the biggest in the world.

From the start, Sir George employed the best, including the finest pilots from France. Soon, a local newspaper was waxing lyrical. In August, 1910, it reported on Maurice Tétard's flight over the Avon Gorge in a Bristol Boxkite:

> On he sped, over rugged rocks and cliffs which spelt doom should his delicate craft fail him, to the Suspension Bridge. Here a picture was presented which will live long in the memory of those that saw it – the wonderful bridge and the aeroplane as gems of modern science in a natural setting of unrivalled beauty ... one began to realise that flying for humans was no chimera of the imagination but an accomplished fact.

It is interesting to note that for the *Bristol Times and Mirror* correspondent, Brunel's bridge, then not yet fifty years old, was a part of 'modern science'.

The rest, as they say, is history. Bristol's contribution to civil and military aviation through two world wars has been incalculable, reaching its apogee in public sentiment with Concorde, still today the world's most elegant and exciting piece of aeronautical engineering. In between were projects to catch the imagination – like the ultimately ill-fated, lumbering Brabazon of the 1940s and '50s, designed to challenge the luxury of the great ocean-going liners. Extensions to get Brabazon into the air made Filton the world's longest runway, and the huge assembly hall built for the new airliner was the world's biggest, too.

Despite a few well publicized VIP flights, though, the Brabazon dream was not to be and it was soon discarded in favour of commercially viable projects like Britannia. But it provided a legacy of engineering experience – through Concorde and beyond – which has kept Bristol in the forefront of the industry right to the present day.

A plaque at Clare Street House, at the heart of the city, was unveiled in February, 1995 to mark the birthplace of

Concorde in production at Filton.

Bristol's aerospace industries – a modest reminder of the immense contribution of a man whose name is all but forgotten in his native city, but during whose memorial service in 1916, flags flew at half mast, muffled bells rang from church towers, trams decked in black crêpe ribbons halted and Bristolians stood bareheaded and silent in the streets.

The Bristol Aero Collection is planning to establish in Bristol the first museum of aircraft production-cum-educational centre in the UK.   The rapidly growing collection already includes replicas of the 1914 Bristol Scout and the 1919 Bristol Babe, a Britannia airliner, Sycamore helicopter, Bristol Bloodhound missile and a mock-up Giotto satellite presented by British Aerospace, along with smaller artefacts, archive and library.   It is hoped that one day a permanent site will be found for them close to the Filton aerodrome where it all started.

At the Industrial Museum, on Prince's Wharf, the Power to Fly Gallery displays all the aero-engines made in Bristol since 1910, and there is a full-scale mock-up of a Concorde cockpit which was used in the airliner's development.   Open: Apr l-Oct 31 Sat-Wed, 10am-5pm; Nov 1-March 31 Sat and Sun 10am-5pm.   Admission charge (except for leisure card-holders, children under 16 and full time students).

A Bristol Bulldog in the 1930s.

Harveys Wine Museum was the First

Britain was given its first wine museum in 1965, when Harveys opened up their medieval cellars in Denmark Street, Bristol for public visits. It was in these cellars that the world famous Bristol Cream sherry was first named in 1860. The museum houses one of the finest collections of wine glasses, decanters, labels and wine antiques in the country. Visitors can see the early leather bottles and earthenware jugs used for Elizabethan 'sack' and the wares of Bristol's famous glass manufacturer, Henry Ricketts.

Drinking glasses are exceptionally well represented, with a fine collection of early English lead crystal and, of course, superlative examples of the famous Bristol blue glass made in the city by Isaac Jacobs. The final stop in the tour is a reconstructed Elizabethan tavern with a collection of furniture, drinking vessels and china from the sixteenth century onwards.

Harveys' cellars are typical of the underground warrens which permeate vast areas of the city centre. For many years, carts were banned in Bristol streets, for fear the concentrated weight of their wheels might cause the cellar roofs to collapse onto the valuable merchandise below. Instead, sledges were used to drag goods around the city.

The Unicorn Inn at Harveys wine museum.

There are regular guided tours with tutored tastings: telephone 0117 927 5036. Open: Mon-Sat, 10am-5pm. Admission charge. The shop is open to non-museum visitors.

The Sailors' Friend

Countless merchant seamen the world over have owed their lives to a Bristol man, without realising it for one moment. Samuel Plimsoll, born at 9 Colston Parade, behind St Mary Redcliffe church, in 1824, gave his name to the Plimsoll line, the compulsory load line on cargo ships designed to prevent overloading, and the risk of disaster which this would mean.

Plimsoll spent his early working life as a solicitor's clerk and manager of a Bristol brewery. In 1853, he became established in London as a coal merchant, and seeing at first hand the scandal of dangerously overloading colliers led him to campaign for greater safety at sea. He became a Radical MP for Derby in 1868 and had barely set foot in Westminster before he was in bitter conflict with the ship-owners. He introduced a resolution in 1870 condemning the unnecessary loss of life and property in 'coffin ships' but his tireless efforts were not rewarded until the Merchant Shipping Act of 1876.

Plimsoll was what today would be called a 'single issue' campaigner. Four years after the act was passed, he resigned his parliamentary seat but continued to campaign, at considerable personal expense, for the interests of the British sailor. A benign-looking bust stands by the water's edge in Hotwells and there is a plaque to his memory near Neptune's statue at the Bridge Head on the Centre.

Samuel Plimsoll: the unknown sailors' friend.

First for Leaning Towers

It might not match Pisa's more famous campanile, but Bristol's leaning tower can claim to have started leaning first! The off-vertical Gothic tower of Temple Church is a curious landmark for visitors travelling from Temple Meads railway station along Victoria Street to Bristol Bridge.

Although Temple Church was gutted in the blitz, bomb damage isn't to blame for the tilt – the trouble started when the former Knights Templar church was replaced in the 1390s. The foundations of the new church laid in soft alluvial soil were too weak to carry the weight of the new stonework, and the base of the tower started to lean from the outset. The error was partially corrected when an upper stage was added in 1460, at an angle slightly less out of true.

A late medieval brass chandelier – rated the finest in England – which once hung in Temple Church is now to be seen in Bristol Cathedral, and its magnificent Baroque ironwork by the master Bristol smith, William Edney, now graces the Lord Mayor's Chapel on College Green.

The Lord Mayor's Chapel itself is one of those rarities – a church owned by a local council. It is a beautiful, long narrow building dating partly from the thirteenth century, and was originally the church of the Hospital of St Mark. Among the notable contents are splendid effigies and medieval tombs, the Edney ironwork and beautiful medieval and Renaissance glass, the latter bought and installed by Bristol Corporation in the 1820s, some of it from William Beckford's great collection at Fonthill Abbey.

Leaning before Pisa.

England's Finest Norman Chapter House

The vaulted Norman chapter house in Bristol Cathedral, dating from around 1150, is widely recognized as the finest in England. But this is only one of many superlative architectural features and rarities to be found here. All were well documented in Bryan Little's *Churches in Bristol*, a study which prompted Sir John Betjeman at the time to write to the publishers with the plea that other cities could have such booklets.

Among the treasures are a late-medieval brass chandelier and two silver candlesticks, of 1712, given by a promoter of the privateering voyage under Woodes Rogers, a resi-

Breathtaking Norman architecture.

One of the finest church chandeliers in the country.

dent of nearby Queen Square, who rescued Alexander Selkirk and gave Daniel Defoe much material for *Robinson Crusoe*. Also notable are the late-Saxon sculpture of Christ harrowing hell, and many medieval, Elizabethan and later effigies and monuments.

The building's architectural glories, though, are the choir and aisles and the beautiful eastern Lady Chapel. Its set of tomb recesses, half octagons at the top and with surrounding star pattern decoration, are another rarity, which might have influenced late Gothic work in Spain and Portugal.

Bristol Cathedral, as depicted by T.L.S. Rowbotham, one of Braikenridge's artists whose paintings are a valuable record of how the city used to look. The recent road closure has restored something of the serenity which College Green would have enjoyed in Rowbotham's early nineteenth-century times.

Pew end, Bristol Cathedral.

Bristol and the Birth of Methodism

Among the bustle of Bristol's Broadmead shops is the New Room, built by preacher John Wesley in 1739, later to become the first Methodist building in the world, and more commonly known today as John Wesley's Chapel.

Wesley came to Bristol that year in the footsteps of his Oxford friend, George Whitefield, who had preached successfully in the city two years earlier. Whitefield had asked John Wesley to come to Bristol to take over his work with the poor and especially the miners at Kingswood. On 2 April, 1739 Wesley preached his first open air sermon in the 'Brickfields' in St Philips Marsh to a crowd of three thousand.

Wesley preferred to preach indoors, but his provocative style debarred him from Bristol pulpits. He was forced to find premises of his own, and had commissioned and started work on the Broadmead building by the end of 1739. The chastely simple New Room is today immensely quiet save for the tick of the eighteenth-century clock which once served to time the length of sermons. The box pews are a later addition, as the congregation originally sat on benches, the men segregated from the women by a dividing panel down the centre.

Bristol proved to be an important centre of early Methodism. Living rooms were built above the chapel where preachers could sleep and study. The New Room was also used as a school for the poor, a pharmacy for the poor and a subsidised Christian bookshop. Those rooms are now fitted out as a museum. Wesley gave practical

John Wesley rode a quarter of a million miles to give 40,000 sermons.

help, too, giving away most of the money he made, feeding the poor and opening a boarding school for miners' orphans at Kingswood.

Outside the New Room is a statue of John Wesley appropriately on horseback. He is reputed to have travelled a quarter of a million miles, mainly by horse, to deliver his 40,000 or so sermons.

The New Room is the oldest Methodist building still in use.

Regular services are no longer held at the chapel, although informal meetings are held from time to time, and there are occasional lunchtime music recitals.

Open: Mon-Sat 10am-4pm throughout the year, but closed on Wednesdays from October-April.

A statue of brother Charles, the hymn writer, stands in the garden on the Horsefair side of the building. Unlike John, who spent little time in Bristol, Charles lived here for twenty years. Among his best known hymns are 'Love Divine', 'And Can it Be' and 'Hark the Herald Angels'.

His home at 4 Charles Street, St James Barton, is marked with a plaque. Along with the adjoining building, the house was being converted during 1997 into an international Charles Wesley Centre, to run courses on his hymns, and to conduct outreach work into the community.

Mr Goldney's Grotto

Architectural follies seem a particularly English eccentricity, and we certainly have more sham castles, fake romantic ruins, gazebos and shell-houses than any other country in the world. The West Country has its fair share, and Bristol can claim one of the most glittering grottoes to be seen anywhere – Thomas Goldney's wonderful creation sunk in the Clifton hillside in the gardens of Goldney House.

Thomas Goldney III was a scion of a family of Quaker merchants whose fortunes were built partly on their international trade. Thousands of exotic shells brought back by their ships from the Pacific Ocean encrust the walls of the Aladdin's cave he spent nearly thirty years – from 1737 to 1764 – perfecting, with virtually no help, except from his gardener and Thomas Paty, who laid the Coalbrookdale tiles on the floors.

To the conch shells, he added Bristol 'diamonds', quartz mined from the nearby Avon Gorge, and the 'rooms' of the cave were further adorned with a River God statue and, in the Lions' Den, statues of a lion and she-lion, rare examples of animals being found in a British grotto.

Goldney was eager to show his handiwork to visitors and, in the lines from Henry Jones' poem, 'Clifton' of 1766:

> ... each congenial guest with joy invades
> The fountains, grottos, and the clear cascades;
> A minor Stow on Clifton's crown we find
> In epic meekness, like its master's mind.

Sea-shells and Bristol diamonds.

Jonathan Holt, who has made a special study of around 200 follies in Wessex, suggests that Goldney's is remarkable as a trend-setting piece of work – little like this had been essayed before, and its creator did not have a land-owning circle of friends to suggest examples; nor did he belong to that aristocratic class which went on the Grand Tour and might have seen the grottoes of Italy on which to base their fancies when they returned home.

Goldney House is now owned by the University of Bristol, and the gardens and grotto are occasionally opened to the public.

Up, up and Away

Bristol's undisputed claim to be the ballooning capital of the world had its beginnings back in 1966 when engineer Don Cameron's small team built the first modern hot-air balloon in Europe. Today, Cameron Balloons are the world's largest balloon manufacturers, turning out on average one a day in Bristol, while a sister company in Michigan looks after the USA market.

Don Cameron had the original idea for Bristol's famed international balloon fiesta, and 1979 witnessed the first massed ascent of balloons from Ashton Court. Balloonists now come from all over the world for this annnual event, held usually on the first weekend in August. It is by far the biggest such event outside the States, attracting around 150 balloonists and half-a-million visitors.

As well as the conventional 'round' balloon, Cameron are famous for their special shapes – the Fantasia Castle for Disney, a space shuttle, shoes, telephone, fruit, golf balls, Mickey Mouse and Donald Duck and other bizarre shapes. All are built entirely of fabric, and there are no solid internal devices to help them keep their shape. Cameron have made around 250 of them, or four out of every five of all the special shape balloons flying in the world.

The Bristol firm have also pioneered the hot-air airship, a dirigible shaped hot-air balloon that can be manoeuvred by a small engine and fabric rudder. Cameron Roziere balloons repeatedly hit the headlines in the 1990s by crossing Australia, making the first solo lighter-than-air flight across the Pacific and setting a new distance record of 10,000 miles, from launch in the USA to landing in India.

Ballooning Bristol.

First for the Millenium

Nothing, they say, succeeds like success. And two great Bristol success stories underpin the exciting new world that began taking shape on the city's harbourside in 1997. Bristol Harbourside, situated right in the centre of the city, brings together the arts and sciences, along with new homes and businesses in Europe's largest inner city regeneration scheme.

With National Lottery backing, Wildscreen World – the world's first purpose-built wildlife and environment media centre – will build on Bristol's success in natural history film making and photography. A large-format cinema with a screen several storeys high will show specially made films, some in 3D, while an electronic zoo will focus on the earth's smaller life forms, blending live exhibits with electronic systems. Magic windows will allow real-life observation of animals in the wild, and in the botanical house, visitors will experience the humidity and smells of different climates. Free-flying birds and insects will inhabit the tropical zone.

The ARKive will be the world's first electronic archive of endangered species, while in the Museum of Wildlife Photography visitors can study the skills and ingenuity of film makers and photographers out in the wild.

Nearby, Science World, the second of the Bristol 2000 projects, will be a leading force in the science centres of the future. Growing out of Bristol's acclaimed Exploratory, it will develop the hand-ons approach which makes today's science accessible and fun for everyone.

Elsewhere on the 66-acre site, and designed to compete with the best of Europe's arts venues, the Centre for the Performing Arts, if it secures National Lottery funding, will open in the year 2001 with a magnificent 2300-seater concert hall and a contemporary dance auditorium seating up to 450. Designed by the German Gunter and Stefan Behnisch father-and-son architectural team, the plans for the CPA building have been memorably described by one commentator as looking 'as if it had been hit by a vorticist force beam'. It is a stunning example of the currently fashionable 'decon' style (short for deconstructionism), bringing a virtuoso international design worthy of the Harbourside vision.

'Hit by a vorticist force beam': model of the proposed Centre for the Performing Arts.

The Bristol Harbourside developments, when completed, will be a triumph for co-operation between the city council, the local business community and the government agency, English Partnerships. This partnership, in which the Bristol Chamber of Commerce & Initiative and the Bristol Cultural Development Partnership have played crucial roles, led to the forming of Bristol 2000 – itself something of a first and likely to become a model for other cities around the country.

Wildscreen World will bring the world's first purpose-built wildlife and environment media attraction to the centre of Bristol.

First for Bristol

This is a selection of two dozen books published by Redcliffe Press currently in print and suggested for further reading. These and other titles are available from local bookshops.

Bristol & Co Helen Reid – profiles of Bristol's oldest firms

Bristol Glass Cleo Witt and others – the story of Bristol's glass industry

Bristol Heritage Fred Warne – a walking guide to Bristol's churches

Bristol Observed Joe Bettey – Bristol through the eyes of visitors down the years

The Bristol Scene Jennifer Gill – nineteenth-century Bristol by local artists

Bristol Seaport Colin Momber – a photographic history of the docks since the 1950s

Brunel's Bristol Buchanan and Williams – the great engineer's work in Bristol

Chronicle of Clifton and Hotwells Helen Reid – the colourful story of genteel Bristol

Church Treasures in Bristol Bryan Little – a guide to church art and artefacts

City Impressions Sheena Stoddard – Bristol through artists' eyes

Design Control in Bristol John Punter – the unvarnished story of post-war planning

Henry Newbolt and the Spirit of Clifton Derek Winterbottom – 'a breathless hush ...'

John Cabot and The Matthew Ian Wilson – Bristol's discovery of America

Loxton's Bristol – Edwardian Bristol depicted by the noted pen-and-ink artist

Mostly Clifton [publication, Autumn 1997] Cedric Barker – a photographic portrait

Pountneys Sarah Levitt – the Bristol Pottery 1905-1969

Quayside Bristol Frank Shipsides and Robert Wall – the story of the City Docks

Restoring the Great Britain Joe Blake – the continuing story

Secret Bristol Downs Geraldine Taylor – a wild-life diary and guide

St Mary Redcliffe Michael Smith – an architectural history of the famous church

Story of Bristol Bryan Little – concise history from the Middle Ages to today

To Build the Second City Tim Mowl – Georgian and Regency Bristol

Tramlines to the Stars George White – the story of early aviation

Victorian Buildings in Bristol Clare Crick – the city's nineteenth-century architecture

Index